6-Week Bible Study
Leader guide

Whispers of Remarkable Women

Deborah Devine

Published by Dowell House Publishing, LLC • ©2021
Deborah Devine

All rights reserved. No part of this publication may be reproduced, distributed, or transmitted in any form or by any means, including photocopying, recording, or other electronic or mechanical methods, without the prior written permission of the publisher, except in the case of brief quotations embodied in critical reviews and certain other noncommercial uses permitted by copyright law. For permission requests, write to the publisher, addressed "Attention: Permissions Coordinator," at the address below.

Dowell House Publishing, LLC
2221 Hampstead Dr.
Columbus, OH 43229
www.dowellhousepublishing.com

ISBN (Leader Guide) 978-1-7362297-4-3
ISBN (Study Guide) 978-1-7362297-5-0

Ordering Information:
Quantity sales. Special discounts are available on quantity purchases by corporations, associations, and others. For details, please visit www.dowellhousepublishing.com/store.
Orders by U.S. trade bookstores and wholesalers. We are listed in the Ingram catalogue.
Used by Permission HCSB
©1999,2000,2002,2003,2009 Holman Bible Publishers.

Unless otherwise noted, all Scripture quotations are taken from the Holman Christian Standard Bible®, Used by Permission HCSB
©1999,2000,2002,2003,2009 Holman Bible Publishers. Holman Christian Standard Bible®, Holman CSB®, and HCSB® are federally registered trademarks of
Holman Bible Publishers.

Cover Designs:
Woman Ima
: Copyright: https://www.123rf.com/profile_fizkes'
Swirls: https://www.vecteezy.com/

Printed in the United States of America

Dowell House Publishing, LLC,
Columbus, OH

EDITORIAL TEAM, DOWELL HOUSE PUBLISHING, LLC

Ashley Dowell
Director, Dowell House Publishing, LLC
Lead Graphic Designer

Landon Tucker
Lead Editor
Content Editor

Rebecca Dowell
Content Editor

Brittany Gray
Production Editor

Laney Fultz
Graphic Designer

Contents

About the Author 4
How to Use This Book 5
Introduction 5

Week 1 ~ Fierce Females ~ *Deborah* 7
Week 2 ~ Divine Reversals ~ *Hagar* 15
Week 3 ~ Rescuing roots ~ *Abigail* 21
Week 4 ~ Encouraging Faith ~ *Shunammite Woman* 27
Week 5 ~ Engaging Eternity ~ *Dorcas* 33
Week 6 ~ Women Who Worship ~ *Anna* 39

Final Words 42
Bibliography 43

About the Author

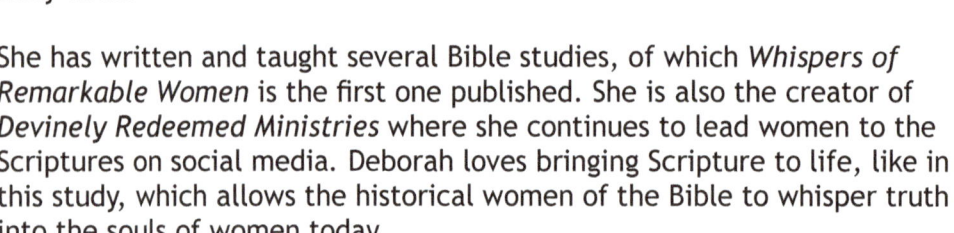

Deborah Devine is a homeschool mother to four children and wife to a full-time pastor in northern Kentucky. If you asked her what she loves most, besides God and her family, she would say, Bible study! She loves leading Bible studies and writing Bible studies. She has a passion for bringing the Bible to life for women who haven't known how to dig in on their own. She enjoys great conversations with women over coffee and encouraging them in their daily lives.

She has written and taught several Bible studies, of which *Whispers of Remarkable Women* is the first one published. She is also the creator of *Devinely Redeemed Ministries* where she continues to lead women to the Scriptures on social media. Deborah loves bringing Scripture to life, like in this study, which allows the historical women of the Bible to whisper truth into the souls of women today.

She currently resides in Williamstown, KY and serves at Sparta Baptist church with her family.

"My deepest desire is for women to fall so in love with Jesus that He oozes from their pores. So if you're ready for a soul cleansing, and an empowering walk with Jesus, then you've come to the right place! I hope you'll find new insights while experiencing the awesome power of our mighty God!"

How to Use This Book

This leader guide is designed to used in conjunction with the Whispers of Remarkable Women Study Guides. Ideally, the small group leader would read through and discuss the points for the week with the participants. During the week, each participant would read through Scriptures and daily devotions before returning to group study time the next week. The key points in this leader guide match up with the fill in the blanks in the "Group Time" section of the study guide.

There are several key sections throughout this book;

1. HISTORICAL RABBITS

Have you ever heard a speaker say they were chasing rabbits? Well, it is a reference to Lewis Carroll's Alice's Adventures in Wonderland where she leaves the set path to follow a rabbit down his rabbit hole. This is the same idea here! Historical context helps us jump into the world of the women we are reading about. If you are looking for a little more context to help the stories come to life, chase some little rabbits with your group!

2. REFLECTION QUESTIONS

> What does Judges 5:7 compare Deborah to?
> (She is called a mother to Israel.)

There are many trivia-type questions that will help the group reflect on the reading. These questions are intended to guide the participants toward key and interesting facts in the story. Who doesn't love trivia?

3. NOTES SECTION

There is ample space at the bottom of each page to write out personal study notes, preparation notes, lecture points, reflection questions, prayer requests, questions to follow up on, and even doodles! We hope you find this section helpful.

Introduction

It is my hope that as we go through this series of Remarkable Women that we can have a newfound appreciation for these women of the Bible and for each other. If we look closely, then we will find pieces of their stories woven into the souls of our own. I love how God uses all sorts of people in different walks of life from ancient days long ago to speak to us even today. If our hearts are open, then we will hear the whispers of wisdom they long for us to discover from their own journeys.

With Love in Christ,

Deborah Devine

MAP OF CANAAN - TWELVE TRIBE PORTIONS

Week 1 - Fierce Females

This week we are going to study the story of the prophetess, Deborah and a warrior of a woman named Jael. I have no doubt you will find these two women were fierce!

First, we need some background! (Please refer to the map on the previous page or in your Study Guide on page 17). If you skim over the first few chapters of Judges, you will notice the author mentions four separate times how the Israelites, "did evil in the eyes of the LORD." Let's begin in **Judges 2:1-4**. Who is being referred to as the Angel of the Lord? "Lord" here is translated "Yahweh" in Hebrew.

> Many scholars believe that the Angel of the Lord is actually referring to Jesus. So, this isn't just any angel! What did the angel of the Lord promise the Israelites in verse 1?
>
> (He promised them land.)

Because of their disobedience, **verse 3** says, "I will not drive out these people before you. They will be thorns [or cause affliction] in your sides, and their gods will be a trap for you."

> Turn to **Judges 4:2**. What did the Lord do to them?
>
> (They were sold to King Jabin of Canaan.)

Why would a loving God do this to his own people? The Holman Old Testament Commentary says it well,

> "It is better to experience some hell on earth
> (with resulting repentance, restoration, and rest)
> than to experience hell in hell."
> (Anders and Phillips, 2004)

Approximately 200 years had passed since the Israelites were freed from the bondage of Pharaoh. The year was about 1200 BC in ancient Israel and the Israelites found themselves in captivity, once again. This period is called the Late Bronze Age, and Israel was unstable. In **Judges 5:6-8** we are told the roads were unprotected and unsecured because there was no longer a central government to do the job. Traveling was dangerous and people were subject to attacks at any time. People had to travel by difficult back roads to go anywhere.

Most of the families were farmers who provided food for marketplaces in the larger nearby cities. Unfortunately, due to the dilapidated trade routes and lack of education, many towns felt an economic collapse that they never recovered from. We even see in verse 8 that no weapons were in the hands of the Israelites. They lacked the technological advancements to make or create their own weapons. The weapons they did have were seized by the neighboring Philistines. In **1 Samuel 13:19-21** we see that the Philistines were experts in metalworking and this put the Israelites at a great disadvantage. The maintenance of their farming tools was controlled by the Philistines as well, and they charged high prices to the Israelites for minimal work.

Judges 4 is centered on Sisera, the Canaanite commander from Harosheth Haggoyim. This location is speculated by many old testament scholars to be located somewhere in the Jezreel Valley. [This area is located around the Jezreel Plain on your map]. The Canaanite oppression of the Israelites was harsh because of Canaan's superior military force, which was led by 900 iron chariots. The oppression lasted for 20 years, and the Israelites experienced some déjà vu as they once again were humbled to cry out to the LORD for help.

In this story we see that God's plan for His people was not bound by the plans of these powerful earthly rulers. He was able to use people who were willing to be used (like Deborah) or simply in the right place at the right time (like Jael) to restore the Israelites to freedom and faithfulness.

NOTES

Read **Judges 4:4-5**

And now we meet our remarkable and wise prophetess, *Deborah*. The culture of that day did not necessarily support a "woman in office". The fact that they had a judicial system in place where Deborah heard the people, made decisions, and implemented the law to various situations meant there must have been a lack of qualified men to do the job. Deborah's palm tree was a well-known landmark then, but of course it is impossible to identify today.

Read **Judges 4:6-9**

Deborah summoned Barak who was from the town of Kedesh in Naphtali. We know that Kedesh (**Joshua 20:2 & 7**) was a city of refuge. Barak's name meant "lightning," however, his decision making wasn't very quick in this text. Barak was called by God through the mouth of Deborah and was considered a leader and warrior. His faith wavered despite Deborah telling

Historical Rabbit:

Kedesh was one of three main cities of refuge or "asylum" at this time that had been set up by God through Moses' obedience in Numbers 35:. The three main cities of refuge were Kedesh, Shechem, and Hebron. God brilliantly chose these three locations because regardless of where a person of Israel lived, a city of refuge wasn't too far of a distance to travel. Each of the cities had remarkably large and strong walls to keep the people inside safe. A person could return to the city they had originally been seeking refuge from only once the high priest in that city died. This is because the death of the high priest meant a new beginning and new life. The Bible always follows this theme: After death, forgiveness is given to the guilty party.

This is the Gospel.

NOTES

Week 1: Fierce Females

him earlier that the victory was his. If only he had realized his calling. God said he would give Sisera into Barak's hands, not Deborah's hands.

God, Himself, promised to hand the Canaanites over to Barak. He was God's chosen man to lead the people out of oppression, but he told Deborah that the **only** way he would go was if she accompanied him.

1. We are sure to be robbed of blessings when we follow God's plan without following God's orders.

Deborah accepted Barak's invitation but revealed he would receive no glory for his leadership. He would have to give that away to a woman. Naturally, he assumed Deborah would be that woman. Since she was so well-known and well-respected, Barak was delighted to share the honor with her! Little did he know that God had another woman in mind for the job. If God calls us to something, I pray we won't be like Barak, who says he will only do it if someone else "better" does it with us. We must feel encouraged because:

2. God never calls us to do anything that He hasn't already planned so that we will always be exactly where we need to be in order to do exactly His will.

We pick up in **Judges 4:10** and see that the tribes of Zebulun and Naphtali were summoned and 10,000 men followed him and Deborah to Mt. Tabor. Let's take just a moment and turn to **Judges 5:13-18** and read these verses, so we can see all of the different clans of the Israelites mentioned.

NOTES

Read **Judges 5:13-18**

They are ALL clans of Israel, but only two answered the call! They were all oppressed by the Canaanites, the Moabites, the Philistines, and others. We can be proud of the Zebulun and Naphtali men in **verse 18** as they are set aside with special praise! They are the first tribes to respond to Barak's summons and call for help. So, what happened with the other tribes? Let's take a closer look.

The tribe of Reuben wasn't as close to the trade routes as Zebulun and Naphtali, so they didn't participate. You can tell in Deborah's song (which is all of chapter 5) that they are mentioned with a hint of bitterness. Like so many Christians today they listened to what God said, took it under consideration, formed a committee, collected research, and then issued a strongly worded statement. They held some sentimentality towards the situation, but not enough to sacrifice for it.

Gilead used to be a heavily wooded area with many springs and gently rounded hills. It is one of the most attractive regions of Palestine. Olive groves and vineyards are sprinkled along the hillsides. It is also the tribal name for Gad as mentioned in **verse 17**. They just simply did not show up.

Dan chose to stay busy with pursuing ships because they were occupied with Canaanites and Philistines to the west. Dan occupied at least some of the Mediterranean seacoast that would have provided an anchorage for small vessels.

Asher was overtaken with Phoenicians at this point in time. Most of the coastline, from Carmel to Tyre, seems to have stayed in Canaanite and Phoenician hands. There isn't much evidence of Israelites even living in the land of Asher during this time up until the time of Solomon.

These three tribes just didn't feel like God's call was important enough for their time or financial burden. It was like a Christian today saying that a struggle within the church or helping a family in need didn't meet their personal needs, so they wouldn't be offering any assistance. It's important for us to understand how much we as people, church members, and sisters in Christ alike need each other. This is just like the tribes needed and depended on one another.

NOTES

As this story continues, you'll notice it's not the victory of just one person that allows the Israelites to succeed. It's coming together and using the gifts that each of them had to offer, which led to peace and rest in the land.

3. Our gifts are offerings to God that we use to display His glory!

We have taken a look at all of the different tribes and those who came to aid Barak in defeating the Canaanites. If we look at our map, then we can see Barak's home in Kedesh of Naphtali overlooking the Hula Valley, about 16 miles north of the Sea of Galilee. However, in **verses 9 & 10**, Kedesh is used as a meeting place. Kedesh (different from Kedesh of Naphtali) is the location mentioned here. It is not on maps today, but was located at the south end of the Sea of Galilee at the foot of Mt. Tabor. From the northern side of Mount Tabor ten thousand Israelites gathered for battle and could spy on their enemy troops. Furthermore, it hid them from the Canaanite forces in Jezreel to the south. This allowed the Israelite men an observational advantage!

Read **Judges 4:11-14**

It's in **verse 11** that we are introduced to Heber, the Kenite. The Kenite's descended from Hobab, an in-law to Moses. In **Judges 1:16**, we read that the Kenites inhabited the area of Southern Judah, but Heber lived beside a large oak tree near Kedesh. We meet Heber here because he was the traitor who informed Sisera (v.12) that Barak and his men were traveling to Mt. Tabor.

As soon as Sisera heard the news, he gathered up his 900 chariot-armed forces and positioned them near the Kishon River passing through Megiddo in the Jezreel Valley and headed for the Plain of Esdraelon. Unfortunately for him, it's at this point that Sisera's line of attack came apart. There was rushing water at the Kishon Riverbed, and the heavy rains turned the plains into mire resembling quicksand. The Kishon River lies south of Mt. Tabor near Megiddo.

NOTES

Although it's a flattened plain that favors the use of chariots, the river's banks were overflowed due to heavy rainfall. Now the Israelites held a strategy with a view!

What does **Judges 5:21** say? "The River Kishon swept them away..." There was a brilliance to luring the enemy into an area where they were overly confident and yet surprised by the condition of the landscape. Normally this territory didn't see much rain. It provided the upper hand the Israelites needed.

Let's finally look at **Judges 4:14**. It's here we read her last words as Deborah charged Barak, "Go! This is the day the Lord has given Sisera into your hands. Has not the Lord gone ahead of you?"

Historical Rabbit

The very next verse is Judges 4:15 which mentions that God "threw" or "routed" Sisera. This is the Hebrew verb that means "to bring into confusion" and it is also the same word used in Exodus 14:24 to explain what God did to Pharaoh's men in the crossing of the red sea.

4. In Judges 5:7 Deborah is called a mother to Israel.

As we wrap up our time with Deborah, I am thankful for the blessing she was to Barak. You see, it was the "children of Israel" who came to her for judgement as she sat under her palm tree. There was no question who would win this battle! Barak obediently advanced, and the Lord brought panic and confusion over all of Sisera's men. Their chariots were wedged in mud,

NOTES

and panic engulfed them. God used human swords and a divine storm to claim victory over Sisera's troops. Deborah announced that the victory was won. She prophesied for the perfect moment in which to attack.

Judges 5:1-7 displays her attitude. She is so grateful for God's hand over the Israelites, and that God allowed her to be a part of such a great triumph!

5. When we allow God to use us where He calls us, then we are overcome with praise!

All she wanted to do was shout and sing praises to the Lord our God! This remarkable woman feared God and her determination to shake the chains of bondage led the Israelites to a great deliverance!

NOTES

Week 2 - Divine Reversals

How often do we try to do God's job? I know I've been guilty of this. We may think we know exactly what we want and how to get it... even if that means not waiting on God and taking matters entirely into our own hands. Are you guilty? I am! Today we look at the story of a remarkable woman who endured the consequences of not waiting on God's promises.

Read Genesis 16

This is the story of *Hagar*. Most of us know her story. She was Sarai's slave. She was from Egypt and since we know in Genesis 12 that Abram and Sarai traveled to Egypt, we can assume that is where they found Hagar.

One of the first things we read in Genesis 16 is that Sarai gave Hagar to Abram as a concubine. During this time period, many men had concubines. A concubine would be a woman who came into the marriage with no dowry or social status. Her entire role and function would be to bear children. Whereas today this seems like a disgusting practice, in ancient times it wasn't uncommon. The barren wife would give her slave girl to her husband and the baby would be like a surrogate child to the barren wife. Despite any type of surrogacy or conception, concubines still had a lower legal standing within the marriage and in society compared to that of the wife.

> ### Historical Rabbit
>
> Most scholars believe Abram and Sarai came in possession of Hagar when they visited Egypt during their trip in Genesis 12. "He treated Abram well because of her, and Abram acquired flocks and herds, male and female donkeys, male and female slaves, and camels." Genesis 16:6

> We see in verse 2 that Abram agreed with what his wife said.
> Does this remind you of any other Bible story?

What about Adam and Eve? Eve gave Adam the fruit and he took it in **Genesis 3:6**. Adam and Abram are both supposed to lead their families. God told Abram that he would bear a son, and it was his job to share that with Sarai and for the both of them to wait on the Lord. Wait and obey. However, the temptation to doubt God and disobey Him was indirectly told/shared with both men all through the manipulation of their wives. Both men gave into what the

women wanted instead of remembering what God said and obeying it! If you read **Genesis 3:17** then God said to Adam, "Because you listened to the voice of your wife." Isn't that exactly what Abram did as well? As important as we think we are, God doesn't need any help from us in order to fulfill His promises!

1. When our faith is abandoned by greed, then we suffer loss of hope in God.
(This was the case for Adam and Eve as well as Abram, Sarai, and Hagar.)

We read in **Genesis 16:4** that Hagar became pregnant and began to treat Sarai poorly. The word used here for despise is *qalal* (kah-lal) and it means to curse someone or to treat them as insignificant. Essentially, Hagar was feeling a little too arrogant in her new pregnant state, and Sarai was feeling a little too jealous.

Interestingly enough, Sarai now blamed Abram for what she demanded him to do. This is just like Adam and Eve all over again. Now Abram is caught weakly in the middle between two women. One he loves and the other is the mother of his child. In the same way, resentment between Adam and Eve was expressed when they hid from each other (**Genesis 3:7**) after they realized their nakedness. Their physical shame affected their deepest intimacy. In this moment, Abram and Sarai became resentful when Sarai confronted Abram for impregnating Hagar. It is clear that Sarai despised Hagar! Just like Adam and Eve, their resentment for one another was the result of sin. Their sins created animosity in their own relationship. Like Adam and Eve, Abram & Sarai would soon see that their sin would be passed down to their children as well.

2. When we attempt to speed up God's plan, then it's possible we'll end up delaying His will.

In verse 6, we see that Abram told Sarai to just do whatever she wanted to with Hagar. Do you think he's being the God-honoring husband and leader of his marriage? I don't believe he is. I believe he's unwilling to handle this situation and therefore drops it into the lap of his wife. Sarai mistreated her in such a way that Hagar felt the only way out of her situation was to run away. Can you imagine? She had just been a servant girl to a woman she admired. Then she was thrust into the arms of that woman's husband only to find herself

NOTES

pregnant. Now she was so poorly treated that she had to run away to escape the suffering inflicted on her by the woman she once adored. My heart hurts for her.

However, I love verse 7! The Angel of the Lord, who was Jesus pre-incarnate, found her by a spring of water in the wilderness and he questioned her. Hagar could outrun Sarai, but she could never outrun God. Don't you find it interesting that throughout this entire chapter God hasn't spoken to Abram once? However, Jesus came and spoke directly to Hagar! This verse is the first mention we see of the Angel of the Lord... Our first introduction to the pre-incarnate Jesus!

Historical Rabbit

It would be remarkably rare in the ancient world for two parties of royalty to greet each other with a message directly. Typically, if a political group wanted to send a message to another group, they would send an ambassador of the group. Communicating directly or face to face would be seen as doing something below themselves. The messenger would speak with authority that was given to him by the King. However, in this passage, Hagar is greeted directly by the King of Kings. Thus, the experience would be shocking and would carry much more weight than if someone came on His behalf.

3. When we are lost, God finds us, provides for us, and redefines us.

The Lord found Hagar. He met her greatest need when He comforted her and heard her distress. Then He gave her hope when he told her she was carrying a son. Sons were a more prestigious gender in the Ancient East. He even gave Her son the name Ishmael. This is what we call a *divine reversal*. Hagar believed she was losing everything, but instead she was visited by Jesus who reversed everything she expected to happen.

The Angel asked her two questions. Where was she from and where was she going? Her answer proved that she knew where she came from, but she had no idea where she was headed. Jesus told her to return to Sarai and submit to her. Submit to her mistreatment. Because she heard God's direct revelation and followed in obedience, then she would be blessed. Hagar stood

NOTES

boldly in direct contrast to Sarai here. Hagar chose to trust God, whereas Sarai tried to take matters into her own hands. What a statement of faith Sarai could learn from her servant girl, Hagar.

Jesus told her if she returned, then her offspring would be more than she could count! Does that sound familiar to you? (If we look over at **Genesis 15:5** then we notice right away that Abram is told the exact same thing about his descendants.) When the Angel of the Lord announced her pregnancy and named her son in verse 11, then this was the first time a pregnancy was announced, and a name given to a baby! Hagar brought us many "firsts" in the book of Genesis. The Angel comforted her because He heard her cry of affliction. Sadly, Ishmael is prophesied in **Genesis 16:12** to behave like a wild donkey and be at odds with his brothers forevermore. We will talk more about that later.

What's even more impressive is that Hagar is the only person in scripture to ever name Yahweh. Not just the only woman. No, she is the only person to give God a name. She named him El Roi. "The God who sees me". She realized what so many of us have yet to learn. We cannot run away from God. He hears our afflictions, and He sees our pain. In verse 15 we see that Hagar obviously returned to the home of Abram and Sarai, because it's Abram, at 86 years old, who named their son Ishmael. I choose to imagine their relationship experienced some restoration. By naming Ishmael, we can conclude that Hagar shared her story with Abram and he believed her.

Read **Genesis 21:1-21**

Next we need to turn over to **Genesis 21:1-2**. Despite Sarah's unbelief, manipulations and mistreatment of Hagar, the Lord blessed her. And 14 years later She had her own son, Isaac. Unfortunately, we see prophesy unravel as Abraham's teenager, Ishmael, treated his toddler brother with malice. Remember in **Genesis 16:12**? Ishmael would be enemies with his brothers. Sadly, **Genesis 25:18** confirms the same thing.

Abraham loved his son as he'd been a part of his life for many years. Nevertheless, there was so much strife between their entire family. The consequences of their earlier sins still affected them. Isaac was the target of Ishmael's scorn. Sarah was distressed over Isaac's mistreatment. Abraham was distressed greatly because of his love for both of his sons. Hagar and Ishmael were surely miserable, because they were ultimately sent away and left to

NOTES

wander around the wilderness of Beersheba. According to ancient law, Hagar is bestowed freedom from her servant status, but in doing so also forfeited any inheritance her son may have had access to. In the face of Abraham's anguish, the Lord revealed to Abraham that it would be Isaac who was the firstborn heir to all of the offspring that God had promised him. However, a nation of offspring was also promised to be fathered by Ishmael in **Genesis 16:10 and 21:13**.

We see that in Genesis 21:15-19 they eventually ran out of water while traveling, and Ishmael was close to death. They were both distressed and weeping when the Lord heard his voice. An Angel of God called out to Hagar, opened her eyes to a well of water, and provided what they needed to sustain them. Once again, God heard them and He saw them. He is *El Roi*, the name given to God by Hagar so many years ago. Proving Himself faithful to her once again.

Verses 20-21 tells us that the Lord was with Ishmael as he grew. Hagar became the first known single mom in history. No doubt she made many sacrifices for her son. She provided for him throughout his life as she helped him find a wife from her heritage in the land of Egypt. Ishmael became the father to the nation of Ishmaelites, known today as the Arabs. Sadly, it's the Arabs and Jews who are still in conflict to this day. Abram and Sarai's sin affected her family for generations to come. In fact, it was an Ishmaelite who took Joseph (her great-grandson) into slavery.

God's word is clear. We must trust Him at His word and wait for Him to fulfill His promises in His timing. Waiting is hard, but we must be patient and endure this life until His promises are fulfilled. Human efforts will not help God along. It's safe to say here that human efforts greatly hindered the life of Hagar.

4. Hagar is the only person in history to ever name Yahweh.

A name we can be so thankful for today! It's because of her that we know the living God, El Roi, sees us and hears us.

> "Since sin is deeper than bad behavior, trying to do better isn't a solution.
> Only grace that changes the heart can rescue us."
> - Paul David Tripp

NOTES

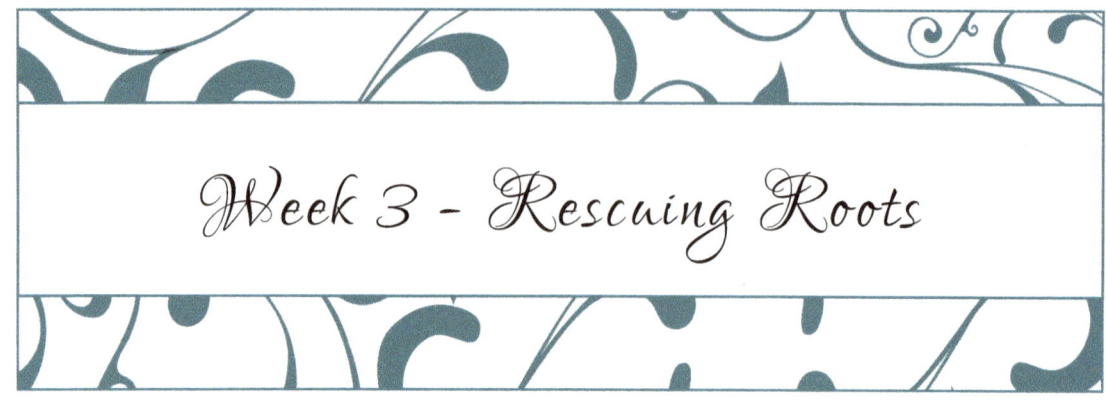

Week 3 - Rescuing Roots

1 Samuel 25:2-42

I know this reading is a little lengthy, but I want you to fully grasp this story and our sweet sister, *Abigail*, and how the Lord used her clever abilities to save a man from self-destruction.

Read **1 Samuel 25:1-3**

> What does Scripture say about Abigail in **verse 3**?
>
> (She is beautiful and intelligent.)

How does Scripture describe her husband, Nabal in **verse 3**? (a Calebite who was harsh and evil in his dealings) If you turn to **Isaiah 32:6** it says, "For a fool speaks foolishness and his mind plots iniquity. He lives in a godless way and speaks falsely about the Lord. He leaves the hungry empty and deprives the thirst of drink." The Hebrew word for "A fool" here is Nabal. While his actual name could be something else, he is known by Nabal to all because of his character. He was a Calebite, part of Judah's clan, and from the same tribe as David. As a descendant of Caleb, Nabal certainly did not reflect his impressive ancestry. (Remember, it is Jesus who will one day emerge from the Tribe of Judah.)

In contrast, Abigail was a beautiful, clever, and blessed woman of God. Some interesting facts about them: Nabal and Abigail are from Maon. Maon was 7 miles south of Hebron (If you look back to page 8 then you'll find Hebron located in Judah.) You may recognize the city of Hebron. It is the place where Abraham considered his home to be and where Sarah died and was buried. It was considered to be a city of refuge and also where David was crowned king. David even made Hebron his home for over seven years. Nabal's business, however, was a few miles north of Maon in Carmel. A city which means God's Vineyard.

Historical Rabbit

Nabal's business was in Carmel, but this isn't the familiar Mount Carmel in 1 Kings 18 where God strikes down the idol Baal. That Mount Carmel is on a mountain range along the coast of Samaria. During this time, Carmel was a great resource for the economic gain in the area because of the ability to breed many animals.

Whispers of Remarkable Women

(v. 2-3) During this time, a man's wealth was measured by his agricultural expanse of livestock and land. Nabal had three thousand sheep and one thousand goats. Wool was a valuable article of trade and served for much of their clothing in those days. With this knowledge, then it's safe to assume that Nabal was a wealthy man.

(v. 4-8) A sheep-shearing festival usually came about once a year between April and May and was a time of rejoicing and celebrating with feasts and fellowship. It was also a time for many men to acquire employment! David heard the festival was taking place, so he sent 10 young men to greet Nabal and offer to help him. David's men agreed to care for Nabal's sheep and guard the other laboring men. When Nabal's men accepted the security that David had offered, then Nabal was now contractually obligated to provide for David and his men. It may not have been a contract on paper. Consider it to be something like two men agreeing on a sale through a handshake.

(v. 7-11) Herdsmen typically received a fee or commission for the services they provided during the shearing festival. David's men were relying on that commission. Normally, reimbursement would include anything like wool, dairy products, or grain. Instead, Nabal, with no intention to compensate David or his men, insulted him and compared him to a runaway slave. He suggested that David was just a nobody. In reality, Nabal was also a thief.

(v. 12-13) David was outraged! He planned to retaliate and kill Nabal with the intention of destroying his family line. David had allowed his anger to get the best of him. In times of stress and hardship, it is easy to explode in anger. Rather than trust God to provide for him and his men, David was focused on revenge. Have you ever been so angry you found yourself focused on the wrong thing?

🐇 Historical Rabbit 🐇

King Saul had a monument of himself made in the town of Carmel according to 1 Samuel 15:12. Some scholars believe that because of Saul's decision to choose the town of Carmel to raise his statue is why so many people in the town adored Saul and seemingly had dissonance towards David in 1 Samuel 25:10-11.

NOTES

Week 3: Rescuing Roots

1. When there is sin, God forms an obstruction to prevent foolishness.

In **1 Samuel 24,** David was the one who had restraint when he was tempted to kill King Saul. However, in **chapter 25** he is now having to be restrained from such temptation by a woman. David was the appointed ruler to Israel. In **2 Samuel 5:2** The Lord states, "'You will shepherd my people Israel, and you will be ruler over Israel.'" David knows he will serve under the Lord's authority. Abigail's reminder of that in **1 Samuel 25:28** brings him back to reality.

Sometimes we can get so caught up in the moment that we "can't see straight." I think that is what happened with both Nabal and David. Furthermore, Nabal's wife, Abigail, received news of the situation. Despite the circumstances, she was full of grace and quickly put a strategy in place. She gathered everything she had available with a plan to stop David in his path. Her goal was to protect her husband and his entire family.

(v. 14-17) We read in **verse 14** that one of Nabal's young men informed Abigail. He traveled from Carmel to Maon, where Abigail was, which was about a mile. He had to leave his work site and travel to Abigail. His role may be small, but his impact was huge! Dale Ralph Davis also said, "We must marvel and adore the God who in His kindness and wisdom leaves no detail untended in his work of delivering his people."[1]

2. The Lord uses those who are committed to dangerous obedience to bring glory to Himself.

(v. 18- 31) Riding a donkey to save Nabal from David's temper, Abigail slid from her animal and fell to the feet of David and begged him for mercy. In the ancient Near East, her proposition was very unusual. Her words are some of the wisest words in Scripture and the longest recorded speech from a woman in the Old Testament. She explained to David that her husband's name summed up who he was. Nabal, which meant fool, truly was a fool. Believing in David's desire to please God, she wisely reached into his soul and brought forth his true nature. His eyes were opened to the truth, and he realized that God had used this humble, generous, and wise woman to stop him from committing the sin of unnecessary bloodshed.

1) Dale Ralph Davis. 1 Samuel: Looking on the Heart. Fearn, Ross-Shire, Scotland, Christian Focus, 2000, pp. 255-265.

NOTES

> What did Abigail bring the men to pay them for their services and satisfy David's anger in **verse 18**?
>
> (She brought 200 loaves of bread, 2 skins of wine, 5 butchered sheep, a bushel of roasted grain, 100 clusters of raisins, and 200 cakes of pressed figs.)

What she took to David is above and beyond what they hoped to receive from their work as bodyguards for Nabal and his men. God truly provided for David and his men. He had demonstrated His provisions to David time and again and He wouldn't let him down now. God desires for us to have pure motives and righteous behavior despite our hardships or personal difficulties.

(v. 32-35) Humbled, David accepted the gifts that Abigail brought to him. If David had continued with his desire to kill Nabal and his family, then do you think he would have been given the blessed title, "a man after God's own heart" in **1 Samuel 13:14**? David realized he trusted Abigail as God's representative. Because he also trusted God then he was able to heed her words of wisdom and lay down his sword.[2]

(v. 37-42) As it turns out, God allowed Nabal's sin to destroy himself. He died 11 days after that encounter from a seizure and paralysis. David remembered Abigail's tender appeal and therefore acted on her behalf by requesting her hand in marriage. She accepted! Their union now allowed David the opportunity to have ties in the area of Hebron near where she lived. Because of this, he could now consult with elders in her part of the country.

3. The Lord promises to secure our destiny when we trust in His providence.

(2) Chisholm, Robert B. *1 and 2 Samuel*. Grand Rapids, Michigan, Baker Books, 2013, pp. 164-169.

NOTES

Isn't it ironic the contrasts between Nabal and Abigail? Nabal died and was buried and Abigail then became royalty! There is divine judgement given to those who mistreat God's people with contempt and hostility.[3]

> **Our God will fulfill the promise of his word. He is on our side. No matter how the wicked strangle, imprison, and persecute, I am the more certain that God is my protection. Our doctrine must prevail; their doctrine must perish. God is our defense; he will see us through whether here or elsewhere. God is our refuge, to him we flee for safety.**
>
> **- Martin Luther (1483-1546)**

David recognized that it was the Lord's providence that sent Abigail to him that day. She kept him from retaliating against himself. David deserves some recognition though. How often does a man actually listen to a woman and take her advice? He sincerely heard Abigail and granted her request. Her intervention on Nabal's behalf demonstrated that she was truly a wise and remarkable woman who sought to honor God.

The Lord didn't ask her to take things to David she didn't have. He didn't expect her to do something she could not do. However, the Lord allowed her to use her gifts and what she had on hand (just like Jael in week 1) in order to save her family and honor God. Abigail contrasts with Eve and Sarai. They went against God and His promises when they advised their husbands. However, Abigail sought God and reminded David of God's promises which led him to repentance."

4. Abigail was a beautiful woman with wisdom and determination.

---

(3) Chisholm, Robert B. *1 and 2 Samuel*. Grand Rapids, Michigan, Baker Books, 2013, pp. 164-169.

NOTES

Week 4 - Encouraging Faith

Shunem was a Baal worshipping people group tucked inside of Israel. Here we find our remarkable woman for today, a prominent woman known only as the *Shunammite Woman*. She's a remarkable woman who was blessed by the prophet Elisha.

Read 2 Kings 4:8-17

Verses 8-10 tell us her husband was quite old, and they had no children. Have you ever known anyone who struggled with infertility? I have several friends who have suffered the misfortune of being either (A) unable to get pregnant or (B) unable to stay pregnant. For the life of me, I don't know which one would be worse. My heart strings are surely tugged tightly around their devastation though. All I've ever wanted to be in my life was a momma. I have had other dreams too, but motherhood was #1, top of the list! To have that dream stripped from me would have been devastating.

The Shunamite Woman's gifts of hospitality as she welcomed Elisha into her home on several occasions. It seems that her faith was one of action. Her husband didn't silence her requests to be a blessing to Elisha by building a room for him.

1. Sowing kindness will reap blessings to our faith.

Verses 11-17 show us that as much as she blessed him, he longed to bless her. While visiting one day, he called her to his room and asked what he could do for her. Elisha held a position of influence within the palace, but her refusal to his request showed that she was content with her household and her life's destiny.

Within her dignity and confidence lay a secret heartache that she alone couldn't speak of. Elisha's servant, Gehazi, unearthed the plight of her deepest fears. Elisha was a man led by God and through the Spirit of the Lord He made her an impressive promise.

> What did Elisha promise her in **verse 16**?
>
> (A child of her own within a year.)

Read 2 Kings 4:18-23

It's important to consider that God does not just help or fulfill promises for the poor and needy. He also cares for those who are fortunate and wealthy. Those with heartbreaks which are just as meaningful and yet often hidden within the recesses of their hearts. God showed her compassion through Elisha.

After her son became ill and died **(v. 20)** then it would seem like her promised blessing was now a broken promise. However, the Shunammite Woman's faith did not waiver. Among a pagan community, she displayed a great faith in God when she asked for a donkey straightaway and one of the servants to immediately go visit Elisha. Her husband didn't understand her mission.

> Look at **verse 23**, What was it that he thought should be happening to warrant a visit to see Elisha?
>
> (A new moon or sabbath.)
>
> The "new moon or the sabbath" found in verse 23 is mentioned because typically in Israel, the common thread was to only interact with prophets on specific days of rest.)

> ### Historical Rabbit
>
> Most scholars agree that verse 19 the boy likely dies from having a sun stroke. The medical field typically agrees that children who suffer from sunstroke do not sweat and usually have temperatures of 105° or higher. If not treated, sunstroke has a high mortality rate in children. This boy truly experienced a resurrection.

NOTES

Whispers of Remarkable Women

The typical theme found throughout the Old Testament is God's promise of province and blessings whenever someone was faithful to God with not only their speech, but the way they lived. The Shunammite Woman is found to be faithful, yet, she's faced with disappointment and hurt. To most of the followers of God, this would have been a devastating blow due to striving to be faithful and usually being blessed, but her faith in **verse 23** elevates how remarkable she is.

Let's turn to **Nehemiah 10:32-33** (if you get to Job then back up 2 books) which says "We assume the responsibility for carrying out the commands to give a third of a shekel each year for the service of the house of our God: for the bread displayed before the LORD, the daily grain offering, the regular burnt offering, the Sabbath and New Moon offerings, the appointed festivals, the holy things, the sin offerings to atone for Israel, and for all the work of the house of our God."

Keyed to their use of a lunar calendar, ancient Israelites marked the first day of the month, with its "new moon" phase, as a festival day (every 29-30 days). As on the Sabbath, all work was to cease (**Amos 8:5**), and there were sacrifices to be made (**Numbers 28:11-15**). In the monarchy period, the king became a prominent figure in these celebrations (**Ezekiel 45:17**). This would have been a convenient opportunity for people to consult a seer or to seek an oracle, which might explain the connection between Elisha and these holy days.[4]

These days were Biblical festival days when Jews would gather together and worship. Supposedly, it's during those times that the Shunammite Woman typically met with Elisha. Her husband was more than likely surprised that she would be seeking him on an ordinary day. However, he also didn't understand the severity of his son's condition. I love her reply to his question. Her faith in the power of God was magnificent as she declared, "Everything will be all right." (**verse 23**)

---

[4] John H. Walton, Victor H. Matthews, and Mark W. Chavalas, The IVP Bible Background Commentary: Old Testament, Accordance electronic ed. (Downers Grove: InterVarsity Press, 2000), 389.

NOTES

2. Our trust in God encourages faith in others.

Read **2 Kings 4:24-30**

According to **verse 25** we learn that she traveled to Mt. Carmel. There's no way of knowing how she knew Elisha's location, but we do know the distance between Mt. Carmel and Shunem is approximately twenty miles. By the time she reached Elisha's location, she refused to be redirected. Dismissing Gehazi and his polite inquiries with another "everything is all right", she ultimately reached Elisha. Her confidence for healing was solely in Elisha, not in Gehazi. She threw herself to the ground and took hold of his feet. We understand about being at the feet of Jesus, right? It's here…at his feet…that she pinpointed her agony. Truthfully, she didn't travel that far just to complain; she went seeking restoration and new life for her son.

This is a great time for us to stop for a moment and reflect: When you go to the feet of Jesus, are you expecting restoration? Ultimately, our God is the God of restoration! It's at his feet that the hemorrhaging woman was healed. It was at his feet that Mary and the disciples sat for Bible Study! It was at his feet on the cross that the ground was soaked with his atoning blood which covered all of our sins. We would do well to remember just how glorious the ground beneath his feet is! Elisha isn't Jesus, but he is the closest thing to God that she can get.

In **verse 28**, we clearly see that her despair for infertility was now turned into torture over the grief of losing her child. This grief was far worse than the sorrow over her infertility. Elisha understood her plea and sent Gehazi to help. He was instructed to tuck in his mantle. Another definition for this in the Hebrew would be to "gird yourself". It's the picking up of his robed clothing and tucking it into his sash/belt so that nothing would hinder his mission. In other words, get ready for battle (**1 Kings 20:11**). Put on your strength (**Proverbs 31:17**). In **Ephesians 6:14** when you're putting on the belt of truth (spiritual armor) then the same expression is used. You are girding yourself. After Gehazi was ready, he was given Elisha's staff, and told to go directly to the boy without any stops along the way. All the while, the woman refused to leave Elisha. Once again, she restated that her faith lay with Elisha. Not with Gehazi or Elisha's staff.

NOTES

Read **2 Kings 4:31-37**

There is no other reference to a prophet being equipped with a staff (the rod of Moses is a different Hebrew word), and the other passages where this word is used speak only of a nondescript stick used for support—often a crutch or cane. From **verse 31** it would appear that Elisha and Gehazi considered it possible that the staff would revive the boy. In Akkadian incantation texts a staff is sometimes the instrument by which exorcisms against the asakku demons (bringing disease and fever) are effected. Since it was the boy's head that hurt, the staff was laid across his face.[5]

Just as the Shunammite Woman suspected, in **verse 31**, the staff was not successful. Elisha finally arrived at their house, went to his room, and found the boy. We were reminded again that the boy is, in fact, dead. Elisha went to him **(verse 33)**, closed the door, and prayed. When things in our own lives feel impossible, then how often do we go to our "room", close the door, and just pray?

Gehazi's failure to restore the boy to life by using Elisha's staff shows that the living God works in response to the requests of trusting people rather than magically through a fetish (Elisha's staff).[6]

Elisha's actions weren't magical. They were the natural, physical demonstration of a man absorbed in sincere prayer. God was so gracious to restore her son's life. Air replenished his lungs, and suddenly he sneezed seven times. Seven! In God's work - seven always indicates completion and perfection. He then opened his eyes. The Lord worked through Elisha to restore this precious, treasured son back to life. Then the Shunammite woman, his mother, was called in to witness his new life.

3. Believers do well to encourage one another with kindness, strong faith, and mutual trust.

(5) John H. Walton, Victor H. Matthews, and Mark W. Chavalas, The IVP Bible Background Commentary: Old Testament, Accordance electronic ed. (Downers Grove: InterVarsity Press, 2000), 390.
(6) Thomas L. Constable, 2 Kings, The Bible Knowledge Commentary; ed. John F. Walvoord and Roy B. Zuck; Accordance electronic ed. 2 vols.; (Wheaton: Victor Books, 1985), 1:546.

NOTES

She fell at Elisha's feet once again and the Hebrew word here for bow is "shachah". Which means she worshipped God at the feet of Elisha. He had given her son a new life! Women were mostly deemed inferior to men in those days, but God showed his love for the Shunammite Woman through Elisha. I have no doubt it was because of her remarkable faith! Her faith is evident all throughout **2 Kings 4**.

4. The Shunammite Woman was a woman filled with encouraging faith and great tenacity.

God rewarded her faith and trust in Him with a surprising birth and an extraordinary renewal to her son's life. Not only was she remarkable... so is our God!

NOTES

Week 5 - Engaging Eternity

Have you ever questioned your own importance? Sometimes in life we can feel so small against the backdrop of this big, hostile world we live in. What do you think would happen if we exchanged our viewpoint for God's viewpoint?

I want to look at a woman whose ministry was small and yet her influence was huge. It's easy to get caught up in the idea that only large, successful ministries are worthy. I hope you'll see that we don't need a huge ministry in order to make a huge difference. Let's read about our remarkable woman.

Read Acts 9:36-42

Our setting is in Joppa. This is where Jonah departed from to escape God in Jonah 1:3. Joppa was one of the most prominent port cities on the coastal plain. It was under Jewish control for about 40 years until Roman Authorities took over in A.D. 6. Despite Roman control, most everyone who lived there remained Jewish. Verse 36 says it's in this city we find the first female disciple, *Dorcas*. Just for clarification: a disciple is anyone who follows Jesus Christ. An apostle would be a follower of Christ who knew Him personally. Even though there were other women considered to be disciples, Dorcas is the only one who Luke calls "mathetria": (mä-thā'-trē-ä) the female version of disciple. It is because of Dorcas that we, too, get to be a mathetria!

> We read in **verse 37** that she died. Where did they put her body?
>
> (In an upstairs room.)

Does that sound familiar to our story of the Shunammite Woman last week in **2 Kings 4**? The boy's body was also taken upstairs for Elisha to heal. Even though Jewish women always washed bodies before burial, we find several parallels in the Old Testament where bodies were kept in an upper room. An attic like room on the flat roof top of homes. Notice her body wasn't prepared for burial though. Usually a body would be anointed for burial with plans to bury the body before sundown. It was never custom for a body to be left unburied overnight.

According to Kaufman Kohler in the Jewish Encyclopedia, "Although the law in Deut. 21:23 refers only to the culprit exposed on the gallows, the rabbinical interpretation derives from it that "no corpse is to remain unburied overnight." With reference to Num. 20:1, it is even urged that burial should follow death closely which Jews felt in the present usage meant: "The burial takes place within as few hours after death as possible". "To keep the dead overnight was not permitted in the city of Jerusalem ". Whether this was due to the climate, which

caused decomposition to ensue rapidly—compare Abraham's words: "Let me bury my dead out of my sight" (Gen. 23:4)—or to the defiling nature of the corpse (Num. 19:11-14), the generally accepted view was that the acceleration of the burial was a praiseworthy act unless preparations for the honor of the dead made delay desirable.

The disciples heard that Peter was nearby in Lydda which is a three-hour trip by foot. It seems like they had plans to call Peter all along. Luke's description of the plea for Peter to come at once causes us to believe they anticipated a miracle...a resurrection, if you will. Peter graciously went to Dorcas and all of the widows approached him telling them of the blessing Dorcas had been to them.

Historical Rabbit

The town of Joppa was about eleven miles away from Lydda. Joppa was built under the leadership of Herod the Great and was seen as the one major port in the Jewish community. Joppa is now known as "Jaffa" and has a population of around 60,000.

Historical Rabbit

Peter stayed at a home nearby after God healed Dorcas according to Acts 9:43. This was the location where God gave Peter a great vision according to Acts 9:43-10:23. The house is about 200 yards from where St. Peter's Church is built today in Joppa.

What was it that Dorcas made for the widows?

(robes & clothes)

NOTES

Through this story, Luke causes us to pause and look at those who seem "unimportant or insignificant". We are presented with the "ordinary" Christians. Those who display the gospel work in their church and community even though applause or recognition is silent against the surroundings of bigger, more distinguished ministries. Making clothes was one of the domestic jobs assigned to women in that culture. Caring for widows was a foundational act of service in early Judaism. Dorcas was their benefactor. In reality, we don't know if she was married. One could argue that since she was always with the widows, then possibly she was a widow herself. Nonetheless, she used gifts given to her by God in order to be a blessing to those around her.

God loves and uses ordinary Christians whose lives may seem to reflect no excitement, no travel, and no fame. Dorcas demonstrates that kind of ministry.[8]

College students are called to particular schools as they feel led into certain professions. God calls some people to be businessmen/women in a money-driven world in order to use their money and influence to share the gospel with those around them. Mothers may have a calling to quit their job/career in order to raise their children. God calls some people to be teachers in their home, in public school, in Sunday school, or in private school. The illustrations are endless and how we are called is trivial. All that matters is God uses different means to reach out to each of His children. Nevertheless, we must be aware of our calling and the Holy Spirit's impression upon our lives in order to be effective for godly living. Dorcas is one of the most remarkable examples we see in the Bible of what it means to be a woman whose heart belonged to the Lord. Are you using your gifts to serve others while also serving the Lord?

1. Everything we do is a form of service to our Lord, Jesus Christ.

In what ways could you be more like Dorcas and serve our Lord?

(8) Kenneth O. Gangel, Acts, HNTC 5; ed. Max Anders; Accordance electronic ed. (Nashville: B & H Publishing Group, 1998), 146.

NOTES

We pick back up in **Acts 9:40**. In accordance with Jewish values, her body would be covered before Peter was ever brought into the room. Notice, Peter sent the others out of the room. Do you see the resemblance once again to Elisha in the story about the Shunammite Woman? It's amazing how God's word is so parallel from the Old Testament to the New Testament. Likewise, we see in **Matthew 6:6,** "But when you pray, go into your private room, shut your door, and pray to your Father who is in secret. And your Father who sees in secret will reward you."

Here we see Peter abiding in the traditions of Elisha... and most especially, Jesus. Similarly, Peter sent everyone out of the room when he emerged to call the dead back to life. He desired to be left alone with the corpse. Like Elisha, Peter fell to his knees in prayer. He sought the only One with resurrection power. Just like the Shunammite Woman's son in **2 Kings 4:35**, Dorcas opened her eyes and was awakened. Just like Elisha gave her son back to her, so Peter presented Dorcas back to the saints. Here we see Peter call her Tabitha, instead of Dorcas. Tabitha is her Jewish name and Dorcas is her name in Greek. Although different, they have the same meaning, "gazelle".

We see many times in Acts how the miracles of God through the apostles attracted a crowd. We can assume that this miracle was no different. This miracle performed by Peter resulted in conversions throughout Joppa! Because Peter traveled to visit saints and was able to heal and raise them as he journeyed throughout the region of Sharon, the light of our remarkable woman, Dorcas, was spread too. Her testimony of caring for those who could not care for themselves was a gift given to all who would listen.

2. If you can't find a place to serve, then create a place to serve.

We all have gifts that we can offer and share with others. This passage isn't one that distinguishes spiritual gifts, but we are definitely enlightened as to how Tabitha used her spiritual gift. Tabitha genuinely practiced the gift of help or service according to **Romans 12:7.**

> "According to the grace given to us, we have different gifts: If prophecy, use it according to the proportion of one's faith; if service, use it in service; if teaching, in teaching; if

NOTES

exhorting, in exhortation; giving, with generosity; leading, with diligence; showing mercy, with cheerfulness."
Romans 12:6-8

Just like the miracles in the Old Testament, Dorcas will one day die again. Unlike Jesus, her resurrection did not equal immortality. Peter temporarily restored her life. In doing so, she could continue serving others and the Lord.

Christians should not try to be somebody else nor to do what God has called someone else to do. God calls and gifts us to be ourselves, even if those selves do not look much like the popular models of a particular era, place, or denomination.[9]

This miracle gave proof to the power of the gospel. It is not in bondage to geography or people groups. This miracle, and others like it, established the authority of Peter as an apostle and opened the door of the gospel to the Gentiles! Peter opened the door of ministry to the Gentiles through which Paul was able to walk through. What a blessing! Peter's ministry in Joppa and the surrounding areas showed his doctrinal authority to move away from absolute Jewish outreach. His ministry was ushered into all people groups. Luke desires for us to understand that Dorcas was the one who helped establish Peter's ongoing significance within the church.

Historical Rabbit

Years earlier, Peter was watching Jesus resurrect a young girl who had died over in Mark 5:35-43. Acts 9:40 provides an eerily similar resemblance to Mark 5:35-43 because Jesus says "Talitha koum" (which is translated, "Little girl, I say to you, get up.") Now a few years later Peter says similar words "Tabitha, get up." In both cases, the women were resurrected.

(9) Kenneth O. Gangel, Acts, HNTC 5; ed. Max Anders; Accordance electronic ed. (Nashville: B & H Publishing Group, 1998), 150.

NOTES

3. The light of Christ longs to open our hearts and use our gifts to influence eternity.

My desire is for all of us to understand the gifts we've been given. May we generously use them to serve others like Dorcas did for her sisters here in Acts.

4. Dorcas was a living testimony that led others to see Jesus.

Let's not diminish any gifts given to us by the Father. We truly don't know the impact that He will establish because of our obedience... Just like in the story of our remarkable sister, Dorcas.

NOTES

Week 6 – Women Who Worship

When you think of the word "Worship", what do you think of? Do you imagine yourself kneeling before the throne in Heaven? Do you see yourself standing in a sanctuary or a concert with hands raised up in praise? Do you think of a time of silence when it's just you and Jesus and your heart is in tune to His Spirit and His presence? This week I want to search the scriptures and look at a woman who truly knew what it meant to worship Jesus.

First, let's consider what does the word worship mean? It's an old English term meaning "worth-ship". It referred to humans actively communicating honor and praise to God because He is worthy of it. It could have been through adoration, thanksgiving, prayer, sacrifice, or making vows. Worship can be in formal activities like attending church. It is the communication of God and His people... The entire process that takes place when people come together.

Romans 12:1 says, "Therefore, brothers, by the mercies of God, I urge you to present your bodies as a living sacrifice, holy and pleasing to God; this is your spiritual worship."

Serving other people & loving them sacrificially is a command given to us by God and even fulfilling that command is a part of worship. Notice that the verse **Romans 12:1** is in the present. That means it is on-going. We don't just worship one time and we are finished. We worship continually through serving God and others.

1. We cannot have service without worship and therefore cannot have worship without service.

Going to church, participating in the service, adoration with songs, reading scripture, giving our tithes, hearing a sermon, and spending time in prayer are all parts of worship. However, true worship is about Jesus, and that begins in our hearts.

I researched some ancient history in the NIV Study Bible on Cultural Backgrounds and found that the Old Testament people in the ancient world believed that the gods had made people as slave laborers. Supposedly, they were tired of growing their own food and taking care of their own needs. People cared for the gods who lived an opulent, pampered lifestyle including food, drink, clothing, housing, etc. In turn, the gods took care of the people, because they had vested interests in doing so. Therefore, it was a codependent relationship of mutual need. This provides the context for understanding temples, rituals, worship, and religious obligation in the ancient world and as we read about the different cultural gods of scripture. However, Israel is called to a far different way of thinking. Yahweh has no needs.

If we asked an ancient Israelite about the word worship, then his simple answer would be that literally, the word means to bow down. Which plainly means to lay prostrate on the ground,

face-down. The book of Proverbs uses the word to portray an image of one stooping under a heavy load. In Near Eastern cultures when you entered before a king or someone whose reverence was due, then bowing was a sign of respect. Therefore, the Hebrew word for worship, Shachah ('shaw-ha'), meant to express reverence or respect to a higher authority.

2. Worship is an attitude.

John 4:24 states "God is spirit, and those who worship Him must worship in spirit and truth." Our heart must always be humbled and bowed down before the Lord. This is what it means for worship to be within our spirits and within the truth of our beings. Psalms 95:6 says, "O come, let us worship, and bow down."

We cannot have one without the other. Worship is not just the physical body—through motions and activities—but in spirit. We must have an attitude within our hearts which acknowledges God and his sovereignty over our lives. Worship must be done in truth—honestly, biblically, and centered on Christ. We see here the difference between religion and the gospel: religion describes humankind's search for God; the gospel describes the way God reached down to humanity.

To worship in spirit and truth means, along with other aspects, to worship God with your life. God is spirit, so we are to worship as one who has The Holy Spirit living in us! "In truth" signifies the complete revelation we now have because of Christ Jesus! Our worship must correspond to the nature of who God is. Therefore, we must worship Him in spirit and in truth.

Where the Spirit is not engaged there is no worship at all.[10]

For Christians, worship means to come into the presence of the Lord. It's not about a fuzzy feeling we get when the music is good. It's about singing/speaking worth to Jesus. Above all, He deserves our admiration and humility. Bowing down isn't just a physical act, but also one within our hearts and spirits.

(10) Kenneth O. Gangel, John, HNTC 4; ed. Max Anders; Accordance electronic ed. (Nashville: B & H Publishing Group, 2000), 78. (Dods, pp. 156-57).

Read **Luke 2:36-38**.

Here we find the remarkable prophetess, *Anna*. In the New Testament we do not find very many women who have been given the gift or title of prophetess. Her name, Anna, is actually the Hebrew name for Hannah which means grace. We also know that she descended from the Tribe of Asher.

Read **Deuteronomy 33:24-29**.

> Do you know what Asher means? Look at **verse 29**.
>
> ("How happy you are, Israel." It means happy!)

The next sentence says, "Who is like you a people saved by the Lord?" I'm telling you... you may feel inadequate, uncalled, unworthy, or insignificant, but who is like you, a woman saved by the Lord? No woman is like you... and there is no God like our God. There is nobody like you, because He made you to be YOU and He is OUR God! Because of Him you are made adequate, you are called, you are worthy, and you are significant!

Read **verse 29** again. The shield that protected Israel in the wilderness and the sword that they boasted in is the same shield and sword He bestows upon us today! I can't help but imagine these words of blessing over the Tribe of Asher are also meant to prophecy for the children to come... including the graceful prophetess, Anna.

We learned in Luke that she was married for only seven years before she became a widow. If she married at the standard age of 14, then she was still a very young woman when her husband died. Now she's been a widow for 84 years and this would put her around the age of 105 years old. What a gift she was! I love the wisdom and beauty of an older woman. I love their stories and I love their advice. I love that for so many of these beautiful women you can look at their faces, in their eyes, and see the Spirit of the Lord all over them.

NOTES

Week 6: Women Who Worship

Isaiah 11:2 "The Spirit of the Lord will rest on Him- a Spirit of wisdom and understanding, a Spirit of counsel and strength, a Spirit of knowledge and of the fear of the Lord." Do you know anybody who reminds you of this? There is no doubt in my mind that this verse personified Anna perfectly!

Jewish and Greco-Roman culture often perceived widows who never remarried as spiritual and faithful. Anna never left the temple complex. (**Luke 2:37**) She stayed in the temple day and night and served the Lord with her fasting and prayers. It was her calling. I envision that she was praying as she heard Simeon bless Joseph and Mary in **Luke 2:33-35**. I assume she slowly unbent her body from the position of prayer and slowly made her way to the Christ child as she thanked Him for coming to this sinful world and began publicly acknowledging Him to all the people there who were looking forward to His arrival. She wasn't ashamed... no, she was grateful!

Luke 1:68 proclaims, "Praise the Lord, the God of Israel, because He has visited and provided redemption for His people." Simeon knew it and so did she! We don't know if she was ever a mother. We know that as a widow she had lived a difficult life of poverty. She didn't have much to give, but she could pray and give praise! So often we think we are too young, too busy, or too old. However, we are never too young, too busy, or too old to stop and worship Jesus who came for the sake of our redemption.

God doesn't require our worship. However, because of our worship, then our relationship with God deepens and fills our own hearts in a way that no thing or person ever can. There is a dedication to Jesus that must take priority over everything else in our lives. Above our responsibilities and our obligations.

3. Loyalty to the Messiah requires extravagant worship.

May we give unconditionally and enthusiastically of ourselves like Anna did. Loyalty is expensive and valuable. It may cost us our time, our finances, and possibly our reputation, but we are rewarded with the Lord's peace poured over us, His anointing by the Holy Spirit, and abundant blessings for a life lived well in the presence of our Savior.

NOTES

Next time you approach Jesus, I pray you will worship Him like Anna did. He is the King of kings who deserves our devotion for the holy and reverent King He is. Worship with reckless abandon, full of loyalty and sacrifice. Paul says in Ephesians 6:7 "Serve with a good attitude, as to the Lord and not to men". God used a remarkable woman to uncover His Heavenly purpose which delivered salvation and redemption to His people and for all of the world.

4. Anna was a woman who worshipped with thanksgiving in spirit and in truth.

No matter our age or circumstance, may we pray to the Lord and grant Him worship and thanksgiving for coming to redeem us.

NOTES

What a blessing it has been to gather with you each week and sit at the feet of Jesus! I hope the stories of these remarkable women whispered new truths and insight into your life! It was such a joy for me to study and learn so much about them so I could share them with you. I hope you felt the same way. My prayer is that we realize that we, too, are remarkable women... all because of Jesus!

You can continue to journey through the Scriptures with me by following my page Devinely Redeemed Ministries on Facebook.

Much love and many prayers for you, Sweet Friend,

Deborah Devine

Bibliography

Chisholm, Robert B. 1 and 2 Samuel. Grand Rapids, Michigan, Baker Books, 2013, 164-169.

Constable, Thomas L., John F. Walvoord and Roy B. Zuck. 2 Kings, The Bible Knowledge Commentary; Accordance electronic ed. 2 vols.; (Wheaton: Victor Books, 1985), 1:546.

Davis, Dale Ralph. 1 Samuel: Looking on the Heart. Fearn, Ross-Shire, Scotland, Christian Focus, 2000. 255-265.

Gangel, Kenneth O. John, HNTC 4; ed. Max Anders; Accordance electronic ed. (Nashville: B & H Publishing Group, 2000), 78. (Dods, pp. 146, 156-57).

Kohler, Kaufmann. "Burial," Jewish Encyclopedia, last modified August 2021, http://https://jewishencyclopedia.com/articles/3842-burial#anchor3.

Walton, John H., Victor H. Matthews, and Mark W. Chavalas. The IVP Bible Background Commentary: Old Testament, Accordance electronic ed. (DownersGrove: InterVarsity Press, 2000), 389-390.

www.ingramcontent.com/pod-product-compliance
Lightning Source LLC
Chambersburg PA
CBHW040110120526
44589CB00041B/2993